This Candlewick book
belongs to:

‒ ‒ ‒ ‒ ‒ ‒ ‒ ‒ ‒ ‒ ‒ ‒ ‒ ‒

‒ ‒ ‒ ‒ ‒ ‒ ‒ ‒ ‒ ‒ ‒ ‒ ‒ ‒

To J. A. B.

C. B.

**To my niece Eleonora
and my nephew Alessandro**

L. G.

Text copyright © 2011 by Chris Butterworth
Illustrations copyright © 2011 by Lucia Gaggiotti

First U.S. paperback edition 2013

The Library of Congress has cataloged the hardcover edition as follows:

Butterworth, Christine.
How did that get in my lunchbox? : the story of food / Chris Butterworth ; illustrated by Lucia Gaggiotti. —1st ed.
p. cm.
ISBN 978-0-7636-5005-6 (hardcover)
1. Food—Juvenile literature. 2. Nutrition—Juvenile literature. I. Title.
TX355.B97 2010
641.3—dc22   2010003034

ISBN 978-0-7636-6503-6 (paperback)

15 16 17 SCP 10 9 8 7 6 5 4 3

Printed in Humen, Dongguan, China

This book was typeset in VAG Rounded.
The illustrations were done in mixed media.

Candlewick Press
99 Dover Street
Somerville, Massachusetts 02144

visit us at www.candlewick.com

Chris Butterworth

HOW DID THAT GET IN MY LUNCHBOX?

THE STORY OF FOOD

illustrated by **Lucia Gaggiotti**

CANDLEWICK PRESS

ONE of the best parts of the day is when you lift the lid of your lunchbox to see what's inside. Your parents have packed it with lots of tasty things to eat. They probably got all the food from a grocery store—but food doesn't grow in stores!

So where did it
come from *before*
it was in the store?

HOW DiD THE **BREAD** iN YOUR SANDWiCH GET iN YOUR LUNCHBOX?

A farmer planted seeds in spring, and by summer they'd grown into tall, waving wheat with fat, ripe grains at the tip of every stalk.

The farmer cut the wheat with a giant combine harvester and sent it to a flour mill.

GRAINS

The miller ground the grains into flour, and trucks took the flour to a bakery.

YEAST

SUGAR

The baker mixed the flour with water, sugar, and yeast; kneaded it into a soft, squishy dough; and baked it in a very hot oven.

WATER

FLOUR

Out came fresh loaves of bread—ready to send to the store.

Take a bite of the bread in your sandwich— **MMMMMM**, crusty on the outside and soft in the middle!

HOW DiD THE **CHEESE** iN YOUR SANDWiCH GET iN YOUR LUNCHBOX?

Your cheese was once milk that came from a cow. A farmer milked the cows, and a tanker from the dairy came to collect the milk.

1. In the dairy, cheese makers warmed up the milk . . .

2. . . . and added bacteria to make it turn sour and thick.

5. They drained off the whey, chopped up the rubbery curds, added some salt, and pressed them into blocks.

3. Then they added a substance that animals use to digest milk called rennet . . .

4. . . . and it changed again into bits called curds, floating in whey.

6. They stored the blocks for months until the cheese was ripe.

Bite into your cheese—it's creamy and smooth, but tasty, too—and **TiNGLY** on your tongue!

HOW DiD YOUR TOMATOES GET iN YOUR LUNCHBOX?

Last summer, your tomatoes were growing in a big plastic tunnel full of tomato plants.

The sun and the warmth made the plants grow tall and bloom with yellow flowers. As each flower died, a tiny green tomato fruit began to grow from its middle.

Day by day, the plants sucked up water and the tomatoes swelled from green to orange to red.

When bunches of ripe, scarlet tomatoes dangled from the branches, the grower picked them . . .

1. . . . sorted them . . .

2. . . . packed them . . .

3. . . . and sent them to the store.

POP one in your mouth and squish the sweet-sour juice out!

HOW DiD YOUR APPLE JUiCE GET iN YOUR LUNCHBOX?

Last spring, the apple trees in the orchard were full of flowers. In summer, tiny apple buds grew from each flower stalk. The buds kept growing, and by autumn the trees were full of ripe, sweet fruit.

Pickers climbed into the trees and filled their bins with fruit.

A truck took the bins to the juice factory . . .

where sorters threw out any rotten apples . . .

1. Then a machine washed the rest . . .

1.

2. . . . and mashed them in a milling machine (seeds, skin, and all).

3. A huge press squeezed the mash till all its juice ran out.

2.

3.

4. A heater warmed up the juice to kill off any germs . . .

5. . . . and poured it into cartons.

4.

5.

100% 100% 100% 100% 100% 100% 100%

100%

Suck hard on your straw to taste the apple **TANG**!

HOW DiD YOUR CARROTS GET iN YOUR LUNCHBOX?

Last spring, your carrots were growing in a field on a vegetable farm. You wouldn't have seen any carrots then, just long rows of feathery leaves.

As the leaves grew taller in the summer sun, each carrot root pushed deeper into the earth, soaking up water and turning orange. By late summer, they had swelled so much that the top of each carrot poked out of the earth.

Pickers pulled them up.

Then the carrots
were washed . . .

and packed
into trucks.

Bite into your carrot—
see just how **SWEET**
and **CRUNCHY** it tastes!

HOW DiD THE **CHOCOLATE CHiP** iN YOUR COOKiE GET iNTO YOUR LUNCHBOX?

Cookies are made from flour, sugar, and butter—and this one's got chocolate chips in it.

Chocolate starts off as a bean— well, lots of beans, which grow in pods on a cocoa tree.

The pods are picked from the tree. Then they're cut open and the beans are scooped out. These beans are spread out and left to dry in the sun.

The dried beans are taken to a factory—sometimes on the other side of the world.

In the factory, they're cleaned . . . **1.** . . . roasted . . .

2. . . . and ground into a thick, sticky paste.

3. Sugar's mixed in, so the paste gets sweeter, but it's still gritty, so it's squeezed, stirred, melted, and cooled . . .

. . . to make it really smoooooooth (it takes a lot of work to make chocolate!).

4. Finally the chocolate is molded into blocks.

These are made into little chips that will **MELT** in your mouth all over again!

HOW DiD YOUR CLEMENTiNE GET iN YOUR LUNCHBOX?

Early in summer, the trees in the clementine grove were full of sweet-smelling, waxy flowers.

As the flowers died, a tiny green clementine berry began to grow out of each one.

The clementines swelled in the warm sun, turning from green to yellow. By the time cooler winter weather arrived, the clementines had turned orange and were so heavy and full of juice that they made the branches droop.

Pickers climbed
ladders to reach
them. They had
to wear gloves
so they didn't
bruise the tender
fruit inside
the skin.

They washed
them and packed
them, and the grower
sent the boxes
in trucks to the
market.

It's easy to peel a clementine!
Then all you have to do is pop the
JUiCY pieces in your mouth and
bite: most clementines are seedless!

You've eaten it all—from the first bite of bread to the last piece of fruit! It came from fields and farms, from orchards, from groves, and from dairies. So many people helped bring it to you—farmers and bakers, cheese and chocolate makers, pickers, packers, and truck drivers. And now it's all in your stomach, starting to do the job that food does:

helping you grow taller and stronger, and giving you get-up-and-go!

You need more than lunch to make you grow and keep you healthy. Every day you need to choose food from each of the sections on this plate. Most of your food should come from the "fruits and vegetables" and "carbohydrates" sections.

CARBOHYDRATES
These foods fill you up fast and give you the energy to keep going.

FRUITS and VEGETABLES
Your body needs lots of these to keep you healthy.

These foods are just as important as carbohydrates, fruits, and vegetables—but your body doesn't need as much of them.

PROTEiN
These are "bodybuilders" (to help you grow those extra inches).

DAiRY
These are the "bone builders" (they also help your teeth grow strong).

Then there's the stuff you eat for a treat (just a little of these is enough).

FOOD FACTS

Your body is made mostly of water, so you need
at least six drinks a day to keep yourself topped up.
Most of these drinks should be water
(not soda, which has lots of sugar in it).

Your body is growing all the time
(even when you're asleep!). So remember, don't
skip breakfast—it gets your body through the day.

Too much sitting around won't keep
your body healthy. It doesn't matter
whether you chase a ball, your dog,
or your friends—but spend about
an hour a day on the move!

It's good to eat five different kinds of fruits
and vegetables every day.
Why not try a new
one this week?

iNDEX

Chris Butterworth is the author of many nonfiction books for children, including *Sea Horse: The Shyest Fish in the Sea*, winner of a John Burroughs Prize for natural history writing. She lives in Cornwall, England.

Lucia Gaggiotti is a graphic designer, packager, and illustrator whose images of food have been used by many companies. She lives in London.